The
Longeing
Book

JUDY RICHTER

The Longeing Book

Photographs by
SUE MAYNARD

AN ARCO EQUESTRIAN BOOK

PRENTICE HALL PRESS • New York

Published by Prentice Hall Press
A Division of Simon & Schuster, Inc.
Gulf + Western Building
One Gulf + Western Plaza
New York, NY 10023

PRENTICE HALL PRESS is a trademark of Simon & Schuster, Inc.

An Arco Equestrian Book

Library of Congress Cataloging-in-Publication Data

Richter, Judy.
The longeing book.

Includes index.
1. Lungeing (Horsemanship) I. Title.
SF287.R53 1986   636.1′08′8   85-30088
ISBN 0-668-06324-6

Manufactured in the United States of America

10 9 8 7 6 5 4 3 2 1

First Edition

FOR MAX
with Love and Thanks

*Proper longeing gives the horse flex-
ion, suppleness, confidence, calmness,
and handiness. Improper longeing
causes pain, nervousness, excitement,
disobedience.*

—Colonel Paul Rodianko,
Modern Horsemanship

Contents

	Introduction	3
1	Preparation for Longeing	7
2	Teaching the Young or Inexperienced Horse	37
3	Common Evasions and Suppling Exercises	55
4	Work over Cavaletti and Low Jumps	59
5	Work in Long Reins	77
6	The Fresh Horse	97
7	The Tense Horse	103
8	The Tough Horse	109
9	Competition Horses	117
10	Horses Not to Longe	125
	Afterword	127
	Index	129

The
Longeing
Book

Introduction

Work on the longe line can add an important dimension to a horse's education and well-being. Stated very simply, to longe a horse, the trainer stands in the center of an imaginary circle and works the horse around that circle, using a line or rope to maintain contact with the horse. Whoever thought up the idea of longeing horses was indeed ingenious to have figured out a way of working his horse without exerting himself too strenuously.

The word *longe* is derived from the French: a *longe* is a halter, and the verb *longer* means "to run alongside." Longeing in English may be spelled correctly with either an *o* or a *u*. I prefer "longeing" to "lungeing" simply because to me the latter somehow implies disobedience; I visualize horses lungeing and plunging out of control.

The history of longeing is obscure at best. The ancient Greek horseman Xenophon does not specifically mention longeing as a means of training. The first clear reference to it can be found in Virgil's *Georgics*, Latin verses written some two thousand years ago, during the reign of Augustus. Virgil was commissioned to write on the delights of country life and the pursuits of agriculture and husbandry. About longeing he wrote:

> When three summers have passed and the fourth has come, let him begin to run round the circling course, to make his steps ring even, to flex his legs in alternating curves—let him have a hard work out.

In *The Compleat Horseman*, written in 1696, Sir William Hope, Deputy Lieutenant of the Castle of Edinburgh, Scotland, describes longeing as "the true and best way of ordering an unruly colt before backing."

In *A History of Horsemanship*, Charles Chevenix Trench reports that during the eighteenth century there was a marked change in the mental attitude of the rider/trainer toward his horse. Trench quotes Richard Berenger, who himself was strongly influenced by the teaching of de la Guérinière.

> Disobedience in horses is more frequently owing to want of skill in the horseman, than proceeding from any natural imperfection in the horse. In effect, three things may give rise to it: ignorance, a bad temper, and an incapacity in the animal to do what is required of him. If a horse is ignorant of what you expect him to do, and press him, he will rebel; nothing is more common. Teach him then, and he will know; a frequent repetition of the lessons will convert this knowledge into a habit, and you will reduce him to the most exact obedience.
>
> If he refuses to obey, this fault may arise either from a bad temper, dullness, or from too much malice and impatience; it often is the effect of the two first vices, sometimes the result of all. In either or all these instances, recourse must be had to rigour, but it must be

4

used with caution; for we must not forget that the hopes of recompense have as great an influence over the understanding of the animal, as the fear of punishment.

It behoves then every horseman, who would be perfect in his art, to know from whence the different sorts of defences and rebellions in horses proceed.

During this period, apparently, the practice of longeing changed as well. It became more than just a means of working down an unruly colt. Training a horse on the longe line began to be an art in itself and more importantly an integral part of training for most horses.

Over the years, longeing has been included in the classical training of horses at the Spanish Riding School founded in 1572 in Vienna, at the French Cavalry School at Saumur, and at the U.S. Cavalry School in Fort Riley, Kansas. Knowledgeable riders and trainers the world over have been using the longe line for centuries as an important part of their training programs. For a less experienced rider or trainer, longeing is a good way to start acquiring an understanding of the horse's mentality and abilities without having to worry about riding skill. Longeing a horse properly is not easy, but it is easier to do than riding him properly.

PREPARATION
FOR LONGEING

There are several reasons for training a horse on the longe line.

First of all, longeing is an important introductory exercise; it is usual for young horses to be started on the longe line before they are ridden. The principles of longeing are closely related to the principles of riding, so while teaching a young horse to longe, the trainer is establishing his authority over the horse and teaching the animal obedience to his requests.

With older horses, work on the longe line can supplement training under saddle. Even a few minutes of concentrated work on the longe line can make a tremendous difference with some horses.

A third function of longe-line work is simply exercise for the horse. Exuberant horses, especially young horses, are much easier to deal with under tack if they have had a chance to buck and play around on the longe line first. Some horses never outgrow their need for the longe line.

Whenever a horse is worked on the longe line, the trainer should have specific goals in mind. He should make sure the place he has selected to longe his horse is safe: the footing should be good and the area not too open. He should be sure to use the proper equipment: longe line and whip, bitting rig, protective boots, and/or bandages. He must be able to judge how long to work his horse on the longe line and what specific exercises a particular horse is physically and mentally ready to do. Work on the longe line can be very strenuous for a horse. Hence, good judgment is crucial; it is always better to do too little than too much.

Longeing a horse well is truly an art, but anyone serious about training horses can learn to do it well enough to exercise his horse and further its education.

Getting Ready to Longe

Most problems that arise in the process of longeing a horse occur because the proper precautions have not been taken. When working with horses, it is very important to prevent difficulties before they arise (unless you are purposely trying to pick a fight, which will be discussed later). Before longeing the horse, make sure the situation is set up so that everything works for you, not against you. Pay particular attention to the following: *location, footing, safety,* and *equipment.*

LOCATION. In choosing the location for longeing your horse, arrange the situation so the horse does not learn that he can escape or take advantage of you in other ways. A small enclosed area is best. If such an area is not available, often you can make one in the corner of a ring or a paddock by using the two fence lines for two sides of the area and moving some jump standards and rails to form the other two sides. An area of 60 feet by 60 feet, more or less, will suffice. I prefer a rectangular or square area to a round or circular area, so the longe work can include lines and turns as well as circles. With a young horse or a spoiled tough horse, it is particularly important to have an enclosed area. Do not be lazy. Move those heavy jump standards so that it all goes right. Make the effort from the start to do the job correctly.

For older, experienced horses that are familiar with the routine, a corner of the ring or paddock is usually adequate. Even with them, select the corner closest to the barn or in-gate—in short, closest to "home." If you use a far corner of the ring you are setting yourself up to be hauled around and, worse yet, you are *teaching* the horse that he can drag you around.

When selecting an appropriate location consider whether or not the place is conducive to concentration. The physical contact gained when a horse is worked under saddle is lost when he is longed, so it is even more important to foster concentration and communication between trainer and horse. Try to eliminate any distractions such as a horse running back and forth in a nearby paddock. It is not fair to expect a horse to pay attention to his work if there are too many other things going on. So keep distractions to a minimum, particularly when the horse is just starting to learn about the longeing procedure.

Once the horse knows how to longe, often the best way to introduce a neophyte to a new, exciting situation is to longe him first before riding him. For instance, a young colt at his first horse show should longe a while in the least busy place, if possible near his van or trailer. Once he has begun to settle in, move closer to the action and continue the familiar longeing exercise until he is calm enough to be ridden. The familiar routine of longeing will help him relax despite the surrounding commotion.

In certain instances, a large open area is appropriate for longeing a stale or bored horse, say, a horse that has been traveling several weeks on the show circuit with no chance to be turned out. A relaxing jog or canter on the longe line in a big open field can freshen up a stale horse considerably.

If you are longeing a horse every day, not riding him at all, longe him in different places to create some variety in the routine. (Remember, though, that daily rigorous longeing makes a horse very fit, so avoid too zealous a program of daily longeing unless you are purposely trying to develop the horse's fitness.)

To sum up, the appropriate place for working a horse on the longe line depends on the purpose of the exercise; it must be carefully chosen.

TIMING. How long to longe a horse is always a matter of judgment. Young horses should never be subjected to long, grueling sessions on the longe. Mentally and physically, they simply cannot take it. Two-year-olds should not work more than ten to 15 minutes; three-year-olds, not more than 15 to 20 minutes. Likewise, unfit horses should not work very long, five to ten minutes at the outset, and then gradually work up to 15 to 20 minutes. Usually a longeing session of over 30 minutes is too strenuous mentally and physically and therefore is counterproductive. There are specific situations, however, when a horse simply *must* be worked hard on the longe to get him to perform well. These situations will be dealt with later in the book. Bear in mind that it is *always* better to do too little than too much.

FOOTING. A very important feature of the longeing area is the ground itself. It should be reasonably level. Uneven ground is very hard on a horse's legs and may cause serious injury. Hilly terrain makes the longeing a lot more complicated because the horse must constantly adjust his balance as he goes up and down hill. At all cost avoid slippery ground; even quiet horses slip and fall very easily when traveling in a circle. Such a fall can lame a horse for months or even permanently. Many back and stifle injuries occur because of careless longeing on slippery surfaces.

I prefer sand or dirt as a surface rather than grass, which can be very slippery, especially early in the morning when there is a lot of dew. (Dry grass can also be very slippery, especially if the ground underneath it is hard.) The sand should not be too deep, however, since this can cause serious strain to the horse's muscles, ligaments, and tendons. A mixture of 75 percent sand and 25 percent clay about 5 to 6 inches deep is the ideal footing for longeing a horse. Very hard ground is also tough on the horse's legs; constant pounding will surely make him sore. Also, avoid longeing in a dusty area; dust is bad for his lungs and eyes (not to mention yours!). Muddy footing is always hazardous; it is either deep or slippery, and often both deep *and* slippery. If the footing is unsuitable, be sure to modify and curtail the longeing program, or, better yet, if possible postpone the day's work until the conditions are better. A sound, fresh horse, no matter how obnoxious, is better off than an injured horse.

WEATHER. A judicious horseman always takes the weather into consideration when planning his horse's program. A horse will need to be longed longer on a cold, windy day than on a hot, humid day; good-feeling horses tend to be fresher and more unruly in cold weather. Conversely, longeing sessions should be shorter when the temperature is high because the horse tires more quickly. Remember, too, at horse shows that if the wind comes up late in the day the well-mannered horse of the morning may need a few turns on the longe before his late-afternoon class. On the other hand, do not overwork him in the cool of the morning if a hot, humid day is expected, or you may have "no horse" by midafternoon.

SAFETY. Careless longeing can be hazardous for the trainer as well as for the horse. Because horses are usually exuberant when first started on the longe line, most accidents occur at the beginning of the session, as the horse goes out on the circle, bucking and kicking. Watch out that you are not in the way of his heels as he charges away from you. Anyone who has longed many horses has had numerous

11

close calls, and a lot of people have been seriously hurt. Before you send the horse out on the line, have your longe line organized in your front hand and your whip in your back hand (if the horse is going to the left, your left hand is the front hand for the line and your right hand is the rear hand for the whip.) Never, I repeat, NEVER bend over to pick up the whip as your horse is going out on the line. Watch him carefully as he starts up and stay clear of his heels. (When he reverses and goes the second direction, again be cautious; the little break he gets while you are adjusting the equipment for the new direction may well give him a second wind, and he may charge out again on the second circle.)

Unless your hands are as tough and calloused as mine, you should wear gloves when you longe a horse. If he charges away, you have a better grip on the longe line and your hands will not get ripped by the line. Do not wear spurs when longeing. Obviously you do not need them, and they can get tangled up, especially if the horse is troublesome. In short, you have less control over him from the ground than you do when riding him, so it is all the more important to watch him carefully.

EQUIPMENT. If you are planning to incorporate some jumping exercises in your longeing program, you will need cavaletti, standards, and rails.

Cavaletti (the singular is *cavaletto*) are very useful in teaching a horse balance and rhythm, and they provide excellent groundwork for developing a horse's jumping skills. The best cavaletti are made from rails bolted to crossed 4-by-4's (see Diagram on facing page). They are not easily dislodged when bumped by the horse and they can be adjusted to different heights depending on the horse's program (see Figs. 1–4).

The jump standards should be simple single-pole standards that are light and easy to move around, as shown in Figs. 61–64. They should be no more than 4 feet tall. Jumping on a longe line is a difficult exercise in itself, and it is not necessary to jump high to achieve the desired results. In fact, jumping too high only creates problems and fright-

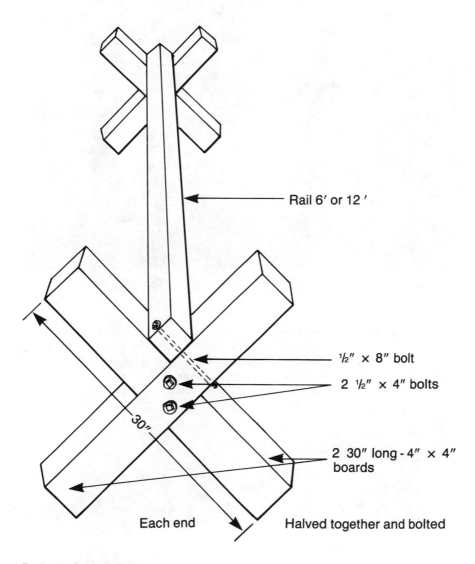

Rail 6' or 12'

½" × 8" bolt

2 ½" × 4" bolts

2 30" long - 4" × 4" boards

30"

Each end

Halved together and bolted

Design by David T. Scott

Fig. 1. Set at the lowest possible height—for beginnings.

Fig. 2. Set at the medium height—ideal for trotting exercises and introductory cantering exercises. For young and/or careful horses, have the rail positioned on the far side of the X. Sloppy horses will become more careful if the rail is on the front of the X. In other words, longe the careful horse over this particular cavaletto on the right circle; longe the sloppy horse on the left circle. Reverse the cavaletti when you reverse the horse.

Fig. 3. Set at full height—mostly for cantering exercises. Some horses are agile enough to trot cavaletti at this height. Oddly enough, there seems to be little correlation between the ability to trot high cavaletti and to jump high jumps with agility.

Fig. 4. Stacking cavaletti like this doesn't work very well. They fall down too easily, with the end result being that the horse learns he can knock jumps down—and if he is real lucky, he gets to rest while they are reset! It is better to use sturdy standards and rails for jumps. If the horse does not respect the jumps from the beginning, he will never respect them.

ens the horse. The purpose of longeing over jumps is to develop proper technique, not to test scope. Short standards put an end, once and for all, to any temptation to make the jumps too high. Furthermore, it is easy to catch the longe line on a tall standard, thereby pulling the jump down and terrifying the horse.

The rails should be 10 to 12 feet in length. Beveled 4-by-4's make good solid rails for the jumps themselves, and can be used as well for ground lines and lean poles. Lean poles prevent the longe line from catching on the standard as the horse jumps (see Figs. 62–65).

Arrange the cavaletti and jumps so that the horse is heading toward the barn when he jumps the first direction. Start with one or two cavaletti and gradually increase the difficulty of the exercise. Once the horse understands the exercise, you can add more cavaletti and a jump as well. Introduce all new material as he heads toward the barn—"home"—to avoid resistance and confusion.

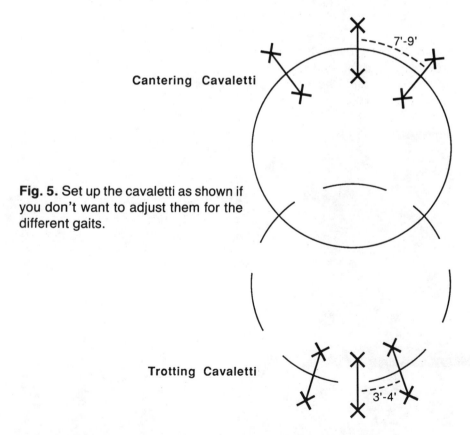

Cantering Cavaletti

Fig. 5. Set up the cavaletti as shown if you don't want to adjust them for the different gaits.

Trotting Cavaletti

Arrange the equipment in the longeing area before you bring the horse out to longe him. Otherwise you run the risk of tangling up the longe line and starting the session off with an alarmed horse. Try to be organized and make everything run smoothly. It is very helpful to have an assistant to adjust the cavaletti and jumps as the session progresses, particularly if the horse is green or spooky.

The Horse's Equipment

The basic equipment needed for longeing a horse includes the following: a bridle (minus the reins) with a thick bit, a surcingle, side reins, a longe line about 30 feet in length, and a longe whip about 9 to 12 feet in length, including the lash. The length of the side reins and their placement on the surcingle is determined first by the age and experience of the horse and second by the trainer's aims and goals.

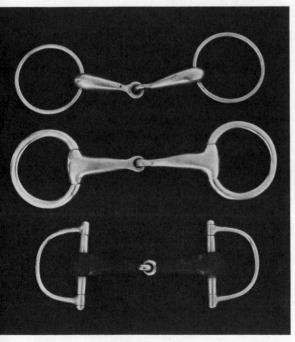

Fig. 6. Here are three appropriate bits to use when longeing. Since a primary reason for longeing a horse is to encourage him to seek the bit, I like to use a thick (rather than a thin and sharp) mouthpiece. I prefer the bit at the top, a loose-ring hollow-mouth snaffle, because it is light and the loose rings allow some play or flexibility. The egg-butt bit underneath it is a good alternative. The bit at the bottom is a metal D bit covered with hard rubber. This last bit, the softest of the three, is just right for starting young colts. (We call it the "gumdrop bit" because they like to chew on it.)

17

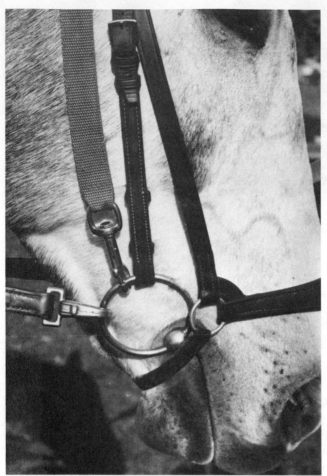

Fig. 7. Horse equipped with a thick loose-ring hollow-mouth snaffle bit, which I prefer for longeing most horses. (Young colts are often happier in an all-rubber bit or a rubber-covered D bit.) It should not hang too low in the horse's mouth or he will play with it too much and possibly even learn to get his tongue over it, a troublesome habit; once learned, it is almost impossible to break. There should be one or two wrinkles in the horse's mouth when the bit is adjusted correctly.

Fig. 8.

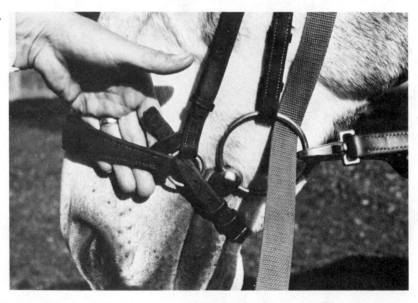

Fig. 9.

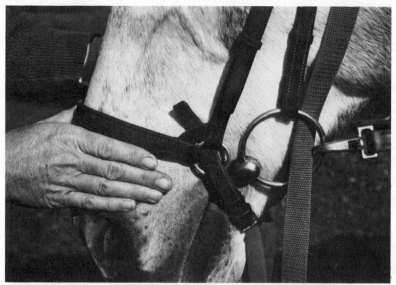

Figs. 8, 9. Either a drop noseband or a regular noseband is appropriate. A drop noseband fastens around and below the bit, but it should not be too low, and unless the horse is very tough, it does not need to be too tight. It should lie at least four fingers above the horse's nostril and you should be able to get several fingers underneath it when it is properly fastened.

Fig. 10. This is a very badly adjusted noseband, guaranteed to pinch the horse's lips.

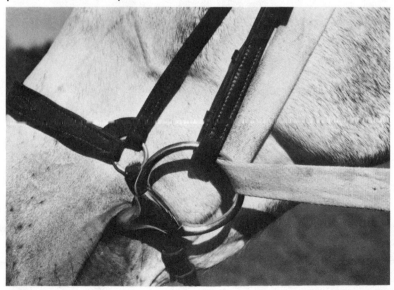

Gear for the horse's legs and feet should include the following: shin boots or polo wraps, bell boots, and hind boots or polo wraps. The boots should fit properly to avoid chafing and the polo wraps should be clean and properly applied. If the ground is slippery and the horse wears screw-in caulks for competition, it is wise to put the caulks in for the longeing as well.

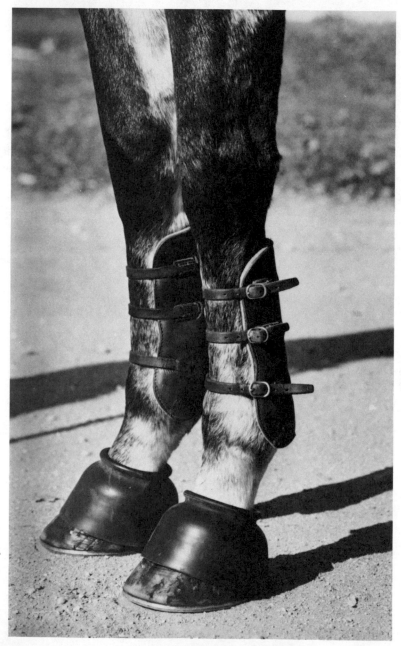

Fig. 11.

Use a surcingle that has a variety of rings (see Figs. 19–22). For the most part, you will want to attach the side reins to the higher rings in order to simulate closely the position of the rider's hands. However, in the case of a very high-headed and/or a very stiff-necked horse, attaching the side reins to the lower rings at first may be more beneficial.

The side reins should be the type made of leather with rubber rings to allow a little "give." Elastic side reins tend to stretch and have too much "give," encouraging the horse to lean against them. In most cases the side reins should be attached to the surcingle at the withers, as shown in Fig. 20, and should be not quite taut as the horse stands with his normal head carriage. With colts I adjust the reins so they are looser, as in Fig. 19, and with old, tough horses I make them tighter, as in Fig. 21. The inside rein, which should be 2 inches shorter than the outside rein, governs the bend of the horse's neck. The outside rein controls his outside shoulder and prevents him from bulging to the outside.

Figs. 17, 18. The side reins I prefer are leather ones with rubber rings sewn in to provide just a little give. If the horse has a very long front, the side reins may be too short. An easy way to lengthen them is to add a couple of double snaps on the withers end of the side reins. (Extra double snaps attached to the bit will clank and annoy the horse.)

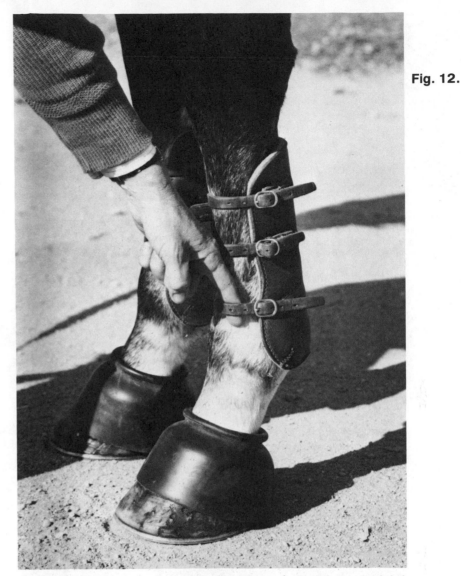

Fig. 12.

Figs. 11, 12. Proper protection of the horse's legs is essential. I prefer these leather open-front shin boots to all other protective leg gear. The tendons and splint bones are well covered by the boots, but the open fronts ensure that the horse who is sloppy over the cavalotti and jumps will be stung by the rails he hits. The top two straps should fit snugly, but the bottom one should be a bit looser to allow freedom to the ankle joint.

Bell boots to prevent the horse from grabbing himself are also essential protective foot gear. I prefer the slip-on variety to those with Velcro closures, which usually do not stay on. The buckle-on bell boots, although easier to put on, are more apt to rub the horse's heels. Slip-on boots go on quite easily if you wet them first.

21

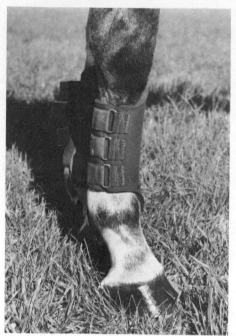

Fig. 13. These shin boots with Velcro fasteners are very handy. They go on quickly and easily and can be removed after work just as easily. When they get wet and muddy, simply brush them off and set them out to dry or throw them in the washing machine (not the dryer, though!).

Fig. 14. These leather hind ankle boots afford sufficient protection to most horses. A few individuals have the tendency to whack their hind legs higher up, and for them polo wraps or full hind boots are necessary. For the most part, I prefer boots to polo wraps. The latter take much longer to put on and they must be put on correctly, not so tight that they stop the circulation, nor so loose that they can slide down. In wet weather they become soggy quickly, and in any weather they usually have to be laundered after each use.

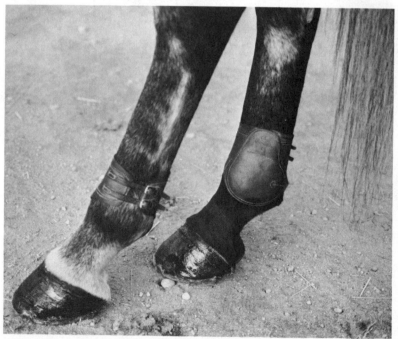

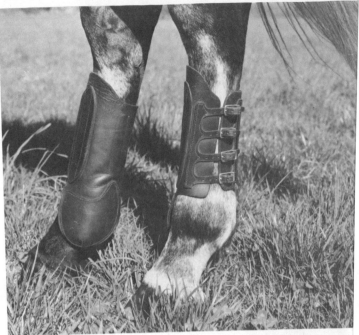

Fig. 15. Here are the full hind boots that offer maximum pro for horses that tend to cuff themselves from behind.

Fig. 16. Polo wraps properly applied. If put on too tight, bandage bows will occur; if too loose, the wraps will fall down. They are good, however, for horses with very sensitive skin who get sores from wearing the regular shin boots.

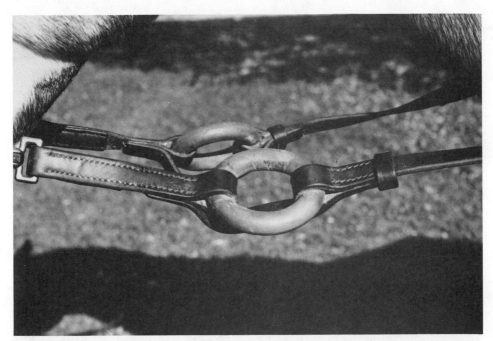

Fig. 17.

Fig. 18.

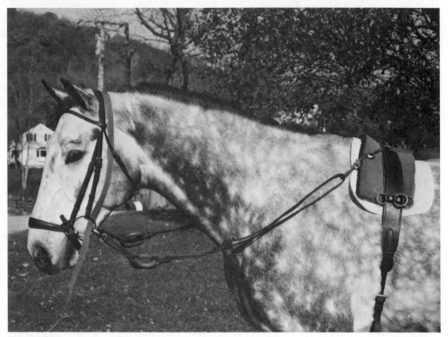

Fig. 19.

Figs. 19–21. There are various rings on the surcingle for attaching the side reins, but in most cases I prefer the top rings because they most closely resemble the location of the rider's hands. If a horse is very high-headed and rigid, or if I have to "get to him" quickly, I sometimes use the lower rings or even put the side reins between his front legs. In **Fig. 19** there is a loop in the side reins for the young horse; they are simply loose guidelines for him. **Fig. 20** demonstrates a good length for longeing a nice horse that carries himself well naturally. **Fig. 21** demonstrates quite tight side reins appropriate for a tough horse that needs to fight himself a bit before the rider gets aboard. Usually I make the inside rein 2 to 3 inches shorter than the outside rein to encourage the horse to follow the arc of the circle.

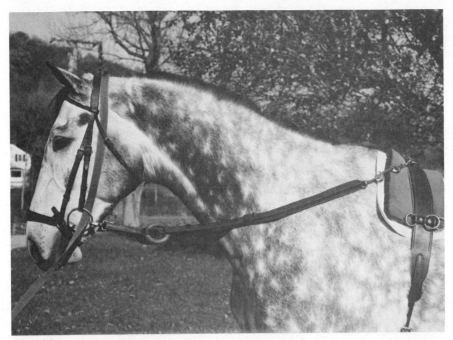

Fig. 20.

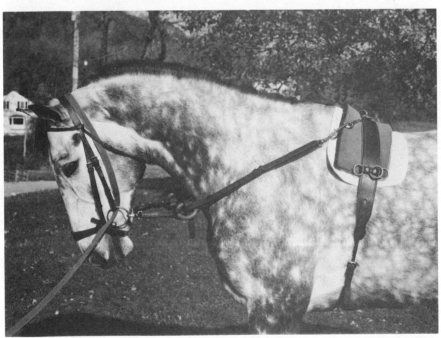

Fig. 21.

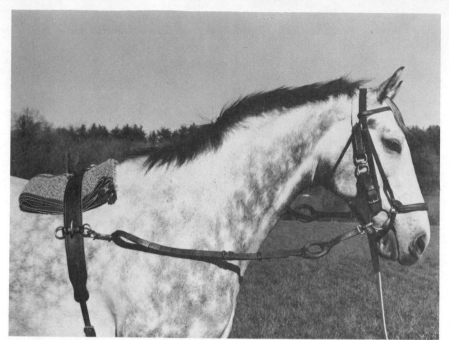

Fig. 22. Here the outside rein is attached to a lower ring to increase control of the horse's outside shoulder. The inside rein is attached to a higher ring.

Fig. 23. Keep the side reins tied up like this when you're not actually working with them. Do not let them dangle down and startle the horse, which can lead to mishaps in the barn. Attach them to the bit after you have reached the longeing area.

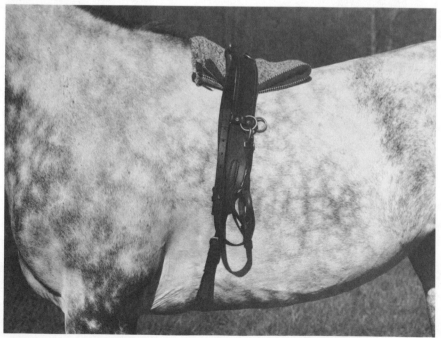

Fig. 24. Here the horse is properly tacked up and ready to longe. The side reins are adjusted to the proper length for a young horse. The surcingle should sit just behind the horse's withers. Use a baby pad next to the horse's skin with a foam pad on top of it to prevent chafing. Tighten the surcingle slowly, but before you start to longe make sure it is really quite snug or it will ride up on the withers, the pads will fall out, and the result will be a frazzled horse with a sore back. Buy a surcingle with a variety of rings on it, since different horses need the side reins attached to different rings according to their head carriage.

Most longe lines are made of sturdy webbing with a swivel snap at one end and a loop at the other. Do *not* put your arm through the loop, for if a horse succeeds in getting out of control, he could drag you by that arm. Some longe lines have a chain at one end. This is handy if you are longeing a horse in his halter, since you can run the chain over his nose for more control. However, the chain attached to the bridle is too heavy as it swings around, and that is enough to bother a sensitive horse.

Fig. 25.

Figs. 25, 26. The longe line should be passed through the bit from the outside to the inside, through the throat latch (to keep it from sliding back), over the poll, again through the throat latch, and down to the bit where it is snapped on the outside. Thus the trainer has control over both sides of the horse's mouth.

Fig. 26.

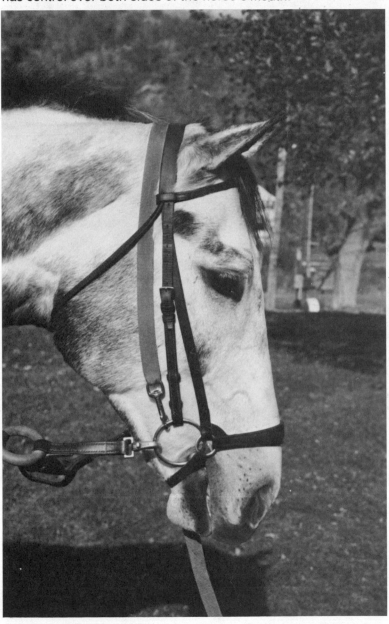

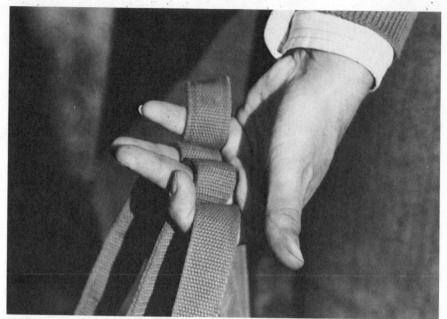

Fig. 27.

Fig. 28.

Figs. 27, 28. If you make a habit of arranging your longe line like this, you will have much better control of your horse and you will be able to increase and decrease the size of the circle without getting all tangled up.

Fig. 29. This rubber disk on the end of the longe line is handy when a horse runs out quickly to the end of the line. It is safer than a sewn loop at the end of the line in case you have to let go.

Fig. 30. When the horse is traveling to the left, the longe line should always be in the front hand and the whip in the rear hand as shown here. Thus you can lead him with the line and follow him with the whip.

Never longe a horse without a proper longe whip. It is as necessary as legs are to the rider; you need it to regulate the horse's impulsion. Think of it more as a driving aid than a punishing device—though it can be the latter if necessary.

So, now, before you start, you have selected an appropriate location, checked that the footing is suitable, made sure that all the equipment is in order, located an assistant

(who, incidently, does not need to be an expert), and outfitted the horse with his proper boots, bandages, bridle,
side reins, surcingle, and longe line and yourself with a
whip. The longeing session should go well because you
have prepared everything properly.

2

TEACHING THE YOUNG OR INEXPERIENCED HORSE

The purpose of longeing a young horse is twofold: to give him exercise, and to teach him obedience. Longeing helps the trainer establish authority and rapport with the horse. Young horses have a short concentration span and their bodies are not yet fully developed, so it is very important not to overwork the young horse. Too little is always better than too much.

Obviously, you will have to proceed much more slowly with an unbroken young horse than with an older horse that has been ridden but does not know how to longe. It is a good idea when working with a new horse to assume that he does not know how to longe. When you send him out on the line, he will either start marching right around you

Fig. 31. "Did you say longe? I don't understand." Puzzlement is written all over his face, so assume he does not know how to longe and start at the beginning. Horses are not at all bashful about showing you what they don't know.

or give you a blank stare, telling you in his own way to explain this new procedure a little more clearly.

In the case of the young unbroken horse—assuming he is halter-broke and knows how to lead—introduce the bri-

dle and the surcingle or saddle gradually and let him get comfortable with them in the safety of his own stall. Be sure he has been turned out for several hours before you even think of starting his education. You want him relaxed, not fresh as paint! Do not let the bit hang too low in his mouth or he will learn straight away to put his tongue over it, a habit that is impossible to break. I do not care for breaking bits with keys on them. I prefer either a rubber D bit or a thick hollow-mouth loose-ring or egg-butt snaffle.

Usually the bit itself is enough of a novelty for a young horse. Adding extra keys encourages him to fiddle too much with the bit. With green colts I prefer to use a longeing halter or a regular halter and chain with the longe line attached to the halter rather than the bit.

Fig. 32.

Fig. 33.

Figs. 32, 33. With young colts I prefer to use a halter and chain shank over the nose, as in **Fig. 32.** The other choice is to attach the longe to the bit as shown in **Fig. 33.** The halter and the chain allow you to maintain control without punishing the horse's mouth if he is rambunctious on the longe—as most colts are. Any colt with eyes as wild-looking as this one's definitely needs to be longed before you ride him, unless you are training him to be a rodeo bronc.

Fig. 34.

Fig. 34.

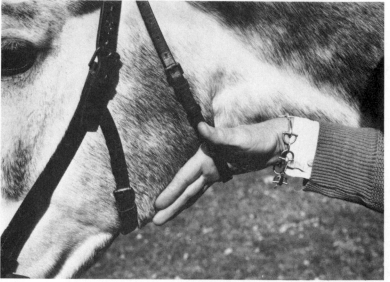

Fig. 35.

Figs. 34–37. The longeing cavesson allows a lot more control than even the chain shank over the nose because of the leverage it gives. Horses that have developed bad longeing habits usually can be controlled with the cavesson, and it is especially helpful when dealing with unruly young colts. Proper adjustment is essential. Adjust to allow one hand's width under the throat latch **(Fig. 35)**, and a couple of fingers under the jaw **(Fig. 36)**. The noseband itself should be very snug or it will slip when you pull hard on his face or when he pulls hard on your hand **(Fig. 37)**. This cavesson can be used alone or with a bit attached when you're teaching a young colt to accept the mouthpiece.

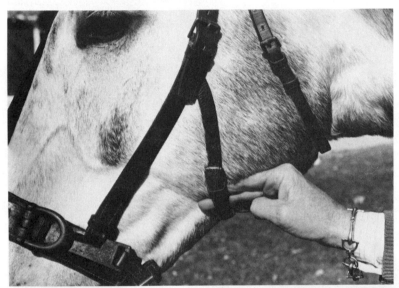

Fig. 36.

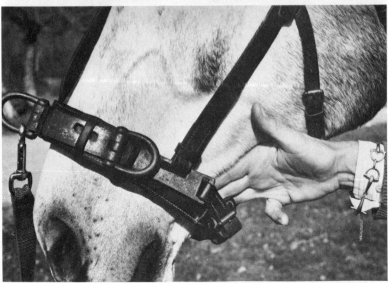

Fig. 37.

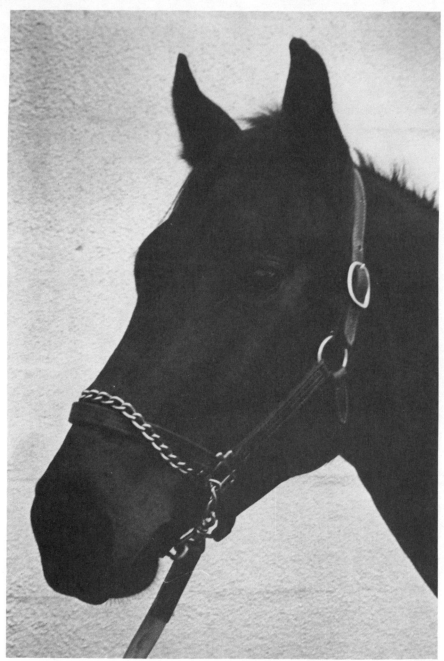

Fig. 38.

Figs. 38, 39. Here is an eighteen-month-old stud colt who is just starting his longeing work. Notice that the halter fits him properly. (If it is too big, it will slide around too much and may even slip off: If it is too small, it will be tight and uncomfortable.) I like to run the chain around his nose and buckle it under his chin. (If the chain is too short, add a double end snap or two to make it fit comfortably.) Even youngsters that have been handled a lot can be pretty unruly at first, and it is very important to have control and establish authority from the start. (A longeing halter affords similar control, but it is too big and cumbersome for colts of this age.) Colts seem to like to spend most of their time prancing around on their hind legs, and like a choke collar on a frisky dog, the chain over the nose gives the trainer the control he needs. Later when the colt wears a saddle and bridle to longe, the halter and chain shank can fit nicely over the bridle to prevent abuse of the mouth until he learns to be more obedient. *(Photographs by Philip Richter.)*

Fig. 39.

Fig. 40.

Figs. 40–42. Here is how to run the chain end of the longe line through the halter ring, around the nosepiece of the halter, and on to the other side, where it snaps on. A chain over the nose assures more control over a fresh horse, and it may make the difference between a safely captive horse circling on the longe line and a loose horse endangering himself and others.

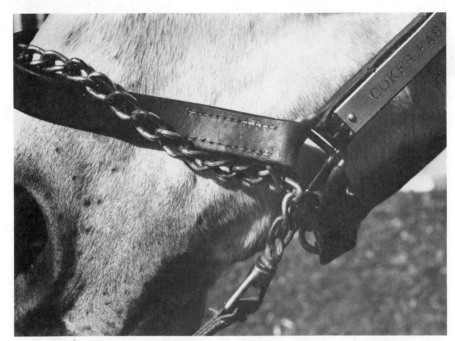

Fig. 41.

Fig. 42.

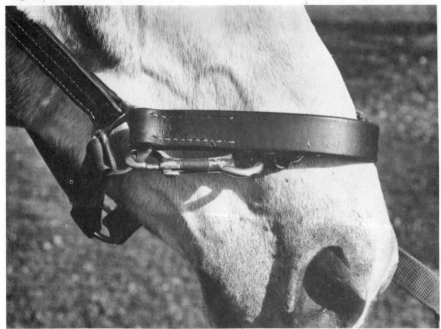

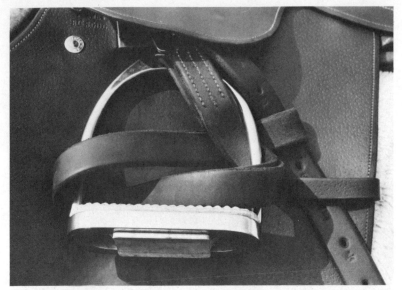

Fig. 43. Tie the stirrups up securely before longeing a horse that is already tacked up.

Introduce the surcingle first by laying a saddle pad or rub rag on the colt's back. If he is not alarmed, lay the surcingle carefully on his back and cinch it up loosely. It will take at least a day or two to familiarize him with the bit and the surcingle. Lead him around with the equipment on, and he will let you know when and how fast to proceed. He may be fine the first or second day, or you may have to repeat the procedure for a week or ten days. Let his reactions guide you.

Arrange to have an enclosed area for longeing until the colt understands what is expected of him. Be sure to have an assistant on hand the first day or two to help you get started. At first, the helper should lead the colt around the circle while you stand in the middle. Have the helper lead the colt from the outside of the circle (that is, on the left circle the helper should be on the colt's right side). Then the helper can gradually step away from the colt without getting tangled up in the longe line. Start right away teach-

Fig. 44. Here is a colt fully tacked up and ready to longe before he is ridden. Most young horses (and many older ones too) are less likely to hump their backs and buck if they have a few minutes on the longe line first. Notice that the stirrups are securely tied so they will not slide down and startle the horse by banging on his rib cage. (In contrast, if you want to be sure to get the bucks out of a lazy colt, leave the stirrups down.) Notice also that the reins are tucked underneath the stirrups. If the horse's neck is very long and the reins short, simply attach the reins to a D on the pommel of the saddle with a double-ended snap or twist one around the other and slip one rein through the throatlatch.

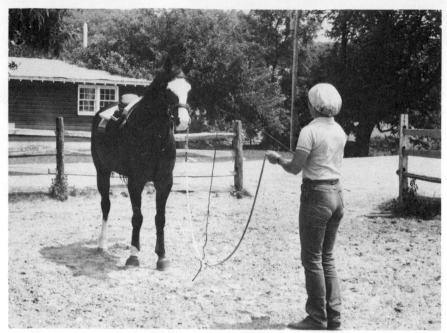

Fig. 45. Here is what *not* to do! Everything in this picture is wrong. The result is that the horse is in charge. His next move could be to step forward and get tangled up in the longe line. More likely he will swiftly turn left and bolt through the open gate back to the barn. Preventing such mishaps is a lot easier than correcting them.

Fig. 46. Here the horse has tried to cut in on the circle and I am preventing that move by pointing the longe whip toward his shoulder. If pointing is not enough, wave it at him or crack it to make your point.

ing the colt voice commands, the cluck and the "whoa," while the assistant is leading him. Reinforce the cluck with a slight movement of the longe whip. The assistant can help stop the horse on the "whoa" command. Once the colt has the idea of walking and stopping, introduce the trot, having first asked the assistant to step away. Again the colt's natural balance and his overall reaction to the lesson will guide you on how to proceed. He should have the walk and the trot down pat before you proceed to the canter.

Fig. 47. Here the horse is trotting freely in a pretty nice round frame. Notice how I am standing slightly *behind* him and following him with the whip close to his haunches.

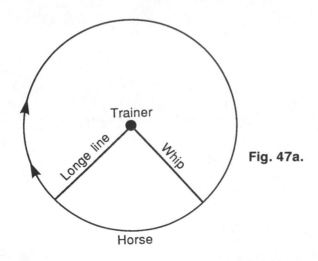

Fig. 47a.

As we said, a young horse's concentration span is short, so do not make the lesson too long: ten minutes more or less working in each direction is plenty for most two-year-olds; approximately 15 minutes is usually enough for three-year-olds. Particularly with young horses, it is always better to do too little than too much. Mentally and physically they are not ready for prolonged concentrated work.

Bear in mind that while on the longe, the horse should be framed between the line and the whip, forming a sort of triangle as he travels around the circle. The horse, the line, and the whip form the sides of the triangle.

Fig. 48. If he has been working in side reins, unhitch the reins and let him stretch his neck and relax as he cools out.

Fig. 49. When you have finished the day's work, bring the horse in to the center of the longeing circle. Take the opportunity to pat him and say a few words to him. Make friends with him without spoiling him.

3

COMMON EVASIONS AND SUPPLING EXERCISES

Common Evasions on the Longe Line

An enclosed area will prevent most longeing problems before they arise. One difficulty is that the horse does not automatically stay equidistant from the trainer while going around on the line. Most horses will cut in on the part of the circle farthest from the barn or home. To prevent that, simply point your longe whip toward his shoulder and soon he will get the idea of staying out on the end of the line. Horses also evade by pulling away from the center— usually on the side toward the barn or home. The fence around him prevents him from actually bolting away and getting loose. If he leans on the longe line, do not lean

55

against the pull. Give and take on the line just as you do when you ride. He must learn to carry himself on the circle and not to be held up by you.

Probably the most common evasion is that the horse charges round and round faster than you want him to go. Again, the enclosed area helps keep him under control. Soothe him with your voice—"easy," "who-o-oa." The tone more than the voice command should calm him. If he charges around to the point of hurting himself or you, it is best to reel him in and lead him around by hand until he regains his composure. (Often this behavior occurs because he has been startled or frightened by something.)

Fig. 50. Here the horse is thinking about hanging back and possibly even balking. I am moving right after him with the whip.

When you start him back on the line, keep the circle small so that he cannot get going.

The most serious form of evasion is for the horse to hide behind the bit or, worse yet, to stop altogether and/or run backwards. A primary reason for longeing a horse is to teach him to go forward and to accept the bit. The longe whip is analogous to the rider's legs and must be used with as much finesse. A very lethargic horse needs to be smacked often to make him go forward. In contrast, a slight flick of the lash is often more than enough to send a sensitive horse forward. There are myriad nuances between those two extremes, and it is a matter of judgment how much to send him forward from the whip. Position yourself slightly *behind* him at all times to prevent him from ever getting behind the bit and behind the whip.

In short, evasions are either lateral or longitudinal. The horse either cuts in or pulls out on the circle, or he travels either too fast or too slow around that circle. Arrange the situation from the outset to prevent those evasions, and you will have less resistance and fewer problems.

Suppling Exercises

Most horses are more supple on one side than the other. Usually but not always the left side is more supple than the right. Most of the horse's attention starting at birth is directed to his left side; he is led on the left side, his blankets fasten on the left, he is mounted from the left side, and if he has been to the race track, all his work has been on the left hand. As a rule of thumb, work him in his easier direction first and his harder direction longer, approximately one-third of the exercise going the easy way, two-thirds going the harder way.

When working the harder direction, you may find that the horse cannot travel as comfortably in a small circle as he can when moving in his better direction. Rather than force the issue, gradually make the circle smaller; if the

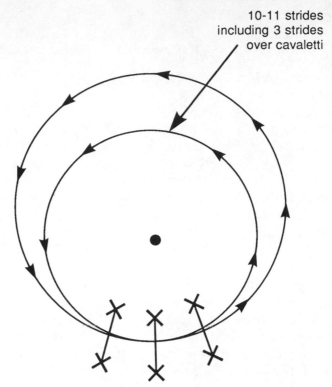

10-11 strides
including 3 strides
over cavaletti

Opening and closing the circle.
(7-8 strides on smaller circle)

Fig. 51. Opening and closing the circle by lengthening and short-ening the longe line. The horse should get around a smaller circle in seven or eight strides, around a larger circle in ten or 11 strides including three over cavaletti.

horse has problems, lengthen the line and let him travel a while on a larger circle. This exercise of opening and clos-ing the circle, making it larger and smaller, teaches him to maintain his balance and rhythm. Be sure that he main-tains a good rhythm as the circle gets smaller. Have the whip behind his quarters to flick at him if he tries to slow down.

Emphasis should be put on transitions among the three gaits—walk, trot, and canter—as well as within these gaits. The working gaits—working walk, working trot, and working canter—should be achieved first. The horse on the longe line should be *working;* there should be liveliness from his hindquarters at all times. Upward and downward transitions from these working gaits should be introduced later.

4

WORK OVER CAVALETTI
AND LOW JUMPS

Cavaletti and low jumps can be incorporated in any longeing program for horses over three years old. Young horses
should become familiar with the longeing routine during
the spring of their two-year-old year, but I prefer to wait
until they are more mature mentally and physically before
introducing work over jumps.

Work Over Cavaletti

Before starting the first day's lesson, arrange the cavaletti
and have an assistant on hand to help after the exercise has
begun. Start with a single cavaletto at the lowest height,

with a second one serving as a wing. Arrange the cavaletti so the horse is heading toward the barn, or "home," when he starts. Work him on the flat first at all gaits; if he is very, very green, lead him at the walk over the cavaletto several times or until he ceases to be astonished by the rail on the ground. An older, mature horse can begin by trotting over the rail and eventually cantering over it.

Once he has mastered one rail, add another, and finally a third and even a fourth. Ideally, it is best to have two sets of three or four cavaletti—four low ones set approximately 3 feet apart and four higher ones set 8 to 9 feet apart, measured from the center of each rail (see Fig. 5). The ends near the center of the circle should be somewhat closer together with the far ends fanned out. With the two sets of cavaletti, one for trotting and one for cantering, you can continually make transitions between the trot and the canter as the lesson develops.

When longeing over cavaletti (and later over jumps), watch the horse as he proceeds around the circle and find the distance to the rail with your peripheral vision. Keep the exercise low and simple until you can be pretty accurate about finding the distance to the cavaletto or the jump. If you consistently "miss the distance" you will just confuse the horse. You *really* have to concentrate when doing this exercise, but with practice you will find that you get better at it pretty quickly. Again I stress the importance of arranging the exercise so you do not have to force the horse to jump. Present the cavaletti/jump to him and let the exercise teach him.

Gradually raise the cavaletti as you become more proficient and as the horse becomes familiar with the exercise. Most horses can cope with the trotting cavaletti at half height. A few finally become agile enough to trot them at full height, a wonderful exercise to strengthen an older horse's back muscles. Many horses simply cannot trot the cavaletti at full height, however, and in this case you should keep the cavaletti at half height rather than trying to force compliance.

Any horse should eventually be able to canter the cavaletti at full height, but do not expect any horse to do the four

Fig. 52.

Figs. 52–58. Here the horse is working at the trot over cavaletti set at the lowest height. Once he has mastered this exercise with two cavaletti, make it more difficult by raising the cavaletti one notch (that is, flipping them over) and adding one or two more to the exercise. (Notice how the extra cavaletti are used as wings at first.)

In **Fig. 52** this horse is pretty high-headed and hollow-backed as he trots over the cavaletti. **Fig. 53** shows a little improvement though he is still fairly inverted. In **Fig. 54** he is beginning to drop his head and relax; he is also getting a little rounder through his back. In **Fig. 55** he is even more relaxed and round. In **Fig. 56** we have changed direction and added another cavaletto. Again he is pretty high-headed and hollow-backed. In **Fig. 57** he is a little softer and rounder but still not as good as he was in **Figs. 54** and **55**, because this particular horse prefers his left side. The final picture **(Fig. 58)** shows further relaxation.

61

Fig. 53.

Fig. 54.

Fig. 55.

Fig. 56.

Fig. 57.

Fig. 58.

Fig. 59.

Figs. 59, 60. Now the horse is cantering the cavaletti at their full height. These cavaletti are about 8 feet apart on the inside and 9 feet apart on the outside to suite this particular horse. Usually, when there is a series of cavaletti, I follow the horse as he goes over them rather than staying absolutely stationary and hauling him around to me. (Notice the barn—"home" to the horse—in the distant background and the split-rail fence in the immediate background. Situating the cavaletti exercise in an appropriate place can make the difference between success and failure of the exercise, particularly when the horse is just learning what to do.)

Here I am working on getting the horse to land on his left head. Standing toward the beginning of the series of cavaletti **(Fig. 59)**, I pull him a bit left as he comes out of the exercise to encourage

Fig. 60.

him to land left. Pulling him hard to make him land on a given lead should be practiced only over cavaletti or low jumps; this, it is hoped, will carry over when he jumps higher. Hauling on his face over larger jumps makes him too worried about his mouth, and as a result he stops using his head and neck when he jumps. Lead him gently left over the larger jumps but don't haul on him. **Fig. 60** shows that the exercise has already carried over. Notice that the cavaletti here are stacked one on top of the other. Another one serves as a lean pole so the longe line won't catch on the end of the top cavaletto. The cavaletti should stack securely one on the other, so they won't topple over if the horse touches them. I prefer to use short, single-pole standards and rails when available.

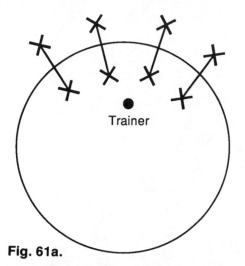

Fig. 61a.

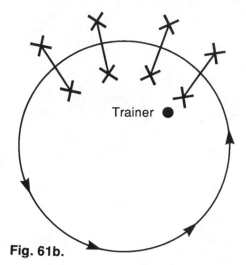

Fig. 61b.

Figs. 61a–c. By moving his position the trainer can tailor the exercise to the horse's needs. **Fig. 61a.** With the trainer in this position, equidistant from all the cavaletti, the horse can comfortably negotiate the exercise. **Fig. 61b.** Trainer is positioned to make the horse turn upon landing coming out of the cavaletti. **Fig. 61c.** Trainer is positioned to make the horse turn sharply coming into the cavaletti exercise.

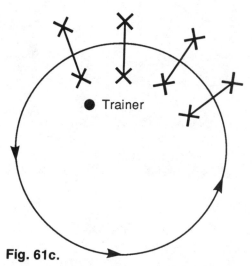

Fig. 61c.

cavaletti at full height on the first day. By the end of a week's practice, however, your pupil should be able to handle the exercise comfortably.

Be sure to have the horse moving forward from behind with his hocks well engaged. Be right there with the whip behind him in case he tries to "back off" at the cavaletti. Keep him in front of you at all times, so that he cannot stop or go the other way. Some horses, on the other hand, try to rush over the cavaletti. With such a horse, soothe him with your voice to try to slow him down; let the cavaletti teach him to be more careful if he charges over them and knocks them in every direction. Keep working the horse until he settles a bit while the assistant resets the rails. After a few such crashes, a horse with any sense should figure out that rushing is not the answer and he had better slow down and be more careful.

To summarize, the two most common evasions at the cavaletti, and also at the jumps when they are introduced, are longitudinal: the horse wants to go either too slowly or too quickly through the exercise. A third evasion—running out—should be prevented before it happens, first by the lean pole, and second by positioning the horse so that he approaches the middle of the cavaletto. He should always have no choice but to march right on through the exercise.

Fig. 62. Joe Jannell longeing his chestnut Thoroughbred gelding Terry Lad at the Cohasset, Mass., Horse Show in the 1940s. A car dealer by profession, Joe was one of the great horsemen of his era. Devoted to his horses, he spent patient hours training them. At home most of his horses longed on command over jumps this big with no longe line whatsoever! *(Photograph by Chester T. Holbrook, courtesy Mrs. M. K. Hofmann.)*

Work Over Low Jumps

Once your horse has mastered the cavaletti exercises, it is time to introduce some simple exercises over low jumps. Usually, I incorporate the jump into the cavaletti exercise because I want to teach the horse to collect himself and jump in good form with his knees up and his back round. The cavaletti teach him to do just that.

Use low jump standards, no higher than 4 feet. There are two reasons for this. First, the longe line is less apt to get caught on a lower standard. (Be sure to use a lean pole to prevent the line from catching on the standard and to serve as a wing.) Second, low jump standards, no more than 4 feet high, remove any possible temptation to jump the horse too high. The primary purpose of longeing over jumps is to improve the horse's style and technique, not to test his scope.

First work the horse over the cavaletti at the trot and the canter. Then build the jump over the third cavaletto so he hops the first two cavaletti, then the jump, and finally the last cavaletto. If the horse is very green, make the jump very low at first—18 inches or so—a crossrail with the third cavaletto at its ground line. An older horse can start at 2 feet or 2 feet 6 inches and work up to bigger jumps. As the jump gets higher, allow more room between the jump and the cavaletto on each side of it. For instance, if at the outset the cavaletti are 8 to 9 feet apart, gradually increase the distances so there is 9 to 10 feet on each side of the jump depending on its height as well as on the horse's stride and level of training. The distance between the first and second cavaletti should remain the same or, if anything, become tighter as the horse becomes more proficient.

Fig. 63.

Figs. 63–66. I rarely longe a horse over jumps higher than 3 feet or 3 feet 6 inches. He can concentrate more on the purpose of the exercise if he is not preoccupied with just getting (or in some cases not getting) to the other side of the jump. To teach him to respect the jumps (and to prevent constant interruptions of the exercise as you reset fallen jumps), use heavy rails and deep jump cups. The lean pole serves two purposes: it discourages the horse from scooting around the jump altogether, and it prevents the longe line from getting caught on the jump standard, a terrifying distraction to a horse. Notice also the location of the exercise. There is a fence between the longeing area and the barn in the background. Most longeing problems can be prevented by using a little common sense.

Fig. 64.

Fig. 65.

Fig. 66.

Fig. 67.

Fig. 68.

Figs. 67–70. Here the jump is somewhat higher and the cavaletti are set farther apart to give the horse a little more room since his arc from takeoff to landing will be bigger and longer. Usually I use standards 4 feet or shorter, since I never jump horses higher than 3 feet 6 inches or 3 feet 9 inches in this exercise. An oxer can be used instead of a vertical in this exercise. It is very strenuous; a half-dozen jumps at each height are usually plenty for the average horse.

Fig. 69.

Fig. 70.

Although the jump itself may be a vertical or an oxer, for the most part I prefer to use a vertical jump with ground lines on each side. The ground lines help the horse judge the distance to the jump. Also, the ground line on the take-off side of the jump allows him time to get his knees up, while the ground line on the far side of the jump encourages him to follow through on the arc of his jump. These ground lines can be adjusted to help develop the horse's technique. For instance, a horse that has problems getting his legs up in front of the jump can be helped by a generous ground line in front of the jump. A horse that unloads his

Fig. 71. Here the horse has overstepped his bounds a bit after the cavaletti and jump. I have followed him over and am hauling him back in on the circle.

legs early needs to have the ground line moved out on the far side of the jump to encourage him to hold his form longer in the air.

Remember to apply all the basic principles of longeing mentioned earlier to your longeing work over jumps. Jump the horse in his good direction first, in his bad direction longer. Since he may not be able to jump in the bad direction as easily, you may have to modify the exercise at first. Build the jump exercise so that the horse is heading toward home in the first direction. Don't discourage him from jumping round by hauling on his head. Be careful to follow the arc of his jump with a good release.

"Jumping round" refers to the bascule the horse should make over the jump. His body should form an arc over the jump ⌒ , not —— or, worse yet, ∪ (head up and back hollow). If he drifts badly to one side or the other, correct it with the lean pole on the rail as well as with the one on the standard. Most important, be sure to keep the longe whip active behind him to make him go forward to the jump.

5

WORK IN LONG REINS

Long reins are a training device closely related to the longe line. The long reins, one on each side of the horse, pass from the bit through loops on the surcingle and back to the trainer. They provide greater control of the horse's hindquarters than is possible with the longe line, and they are very effective in certain instances. My only reservation about long reins is that they are rough on the horse's mouth, especially in the hands of someone who is inexperienced. Hence I recommend that most long-reining, particularly of colts, be done in a hackamore or longeing cavesson rather than in a bit. A horse with an especially sensitive mouth can be long-reined as shown in Figs. 103 and 104 in Chapter 7.

Fig. 72. This horse is properly outfitted in long-rein equipment. An older horse such as this one should be worked in a bit with the long reins.

Long-Reining Colts

The procedure for introducing long reins to a young colt is similar to teaching him how to longe. Spend plenty of time getting him familiar with the equipment. Have an assistant lead him around in an enclosed area until he gets used to the lines. At first, colts are usually pretty skittish about the outside line that passes around the hindquarters. Once a colt is familiar with the equipment on the circle in an enclosed area, you can drive him ahead of you to teach him to go forward and straight. Drive him around the place between jumps, up and down the driveway. Have an assistant on hand to help on the first few excursions. Driving colts around in long reins gives them confidence later when they are first ridden.

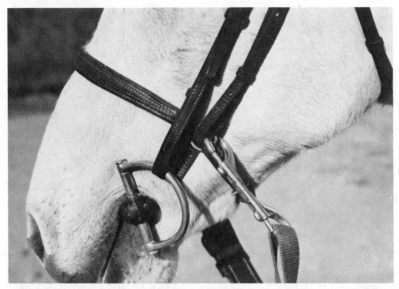

Fig. 73. Here the long lines are attached to the horse's noseband instead of to the bit, a good practice with colts until they learn how to long-rein properly.

Long-Reining Older Horses

Some older horses improve markedly after just a few sessions in the long reins. The big advantage of long reins, as opposed to the longe line, is that they allow tremendous control over the horse's hindquarters. Stiff horses and long, strung-out horses profit most from long-rein work. Use a rubber D bit if you feel the hackamore or longeing cavesson does not afford enough control. Again, start moving the horse around on his good direction first. Keep even contact with both inside and outside reins. Do not let the outside rein slip down off his haunches to his hocks or he may become startled and even kick out and get tangled up in the rein.

Work him on the long reins just as you would on the longe line. Do lots of transitions and practice opening and closing the circle at both the trot and the canter. Have the

Fig. 74.

Fig. 75.

Figs. 74–81. An advantage of the long reins is that the horse can reverse without a major tack change, thus he can reverse often during the lesson. To change direction, shorten the outside rein before you pull on it directly to get the horse to turn. While you tighten the outside rein, let the inside rein slide through your fingers as the horse reverses. Practice the exercise first at the walk and later at the trot.

Fig. 76.

Fig. 77.

Fig. 78.

Fig. 79.

Fig. 80.

Fig. 81.

longe whip in your rear hand to drive him forward if necessary. The long reins afford so much control over the hindquarters that when a horse cross-canters you can force a flying change out of him by holding his hindquarters to the inside and flicking your whip to make him change up.

Horses can also be worked at the trot and canter over cavaletti on the long reins. With the additional control afforded by the outside rein, the rusher can be restrained more effectively. And you will be able to get the horse to land on the correct lead by forcing him to keep his hindquarters under him.

Fig. 82. In this picture the horse shows why he is a likely candidate for the long reins. The arc of his body should correspond to the arc of the circle, but this horse is not even a little bit round. He is just skating around the circle on two wheels, as it were.

Fig. 83. This picture illustrates one of the great advantages of long-reining over longeing. The outside rein is exerting perfect control over the hind-quarters. The horse is slightly bent to the inside; his body correctly follows the curve of the circle.

Fig. 84. Here the outside rein is very active to control the hind-quarters.

Fig. 85. Here at the trot, the long reins help to control the horse's bulging shoulder.

Fig. 86. The long reins are an aid in forcing a horse to land on a certain lead or to do a flying change because they allow so much control over the haunches. This pony was very one-sided when we bought him, and with the help of the long reins we taught him to do flying changes and to land on a given lead. We found that forcing the leads and the changes under saddle just made the pony too strong for a child.

Fig. 87.

Figs. 87–94. Trotting and cantering on the long reins over cavaletti are good suppling exercises. (Do not try jumping the horse in
long reins; his mouth would take too much punishment.) At the
canter over full-height cavaletti (Figs. 91–94) the horse is leaving
the ground a bit too soon and consequently is jumping somewhat
flat.

Fig. 88.

Fig. 89.

Fig. 90.

Fig. 91.

Fig. 92.

Fig. 93.

Fig. 94.

Fig. 95. Here the horse is working nicely in the long reins at the trot. Be careful not to let the outside rein slip too low and startle him.

Fig. 96. Here the horse is working on going *straight* down the lane. Long reins are very helpful in teaching colts not to wander.

Fig. 97.

Figs. 97, 98. Long reins can be used also for lateral work as demonstrated here. In **Fig. 97** the horse's head is bent away from the direction of travel. In **Fig. 98** his head is bent toward the direction of travel. Both are good suppling exercises, the second being more difficult than the first.

Fig. 98.

Fig. 99.

Figs. 99–101. Here is long-reining in its classical and highest form as demonstrated by Lipizzaner stallions of the Spanish Riding School of Vienna during a performance in New York's Madison Square Garden several years ago. In the capriole **(Fig. 101)**, the horse is at the height of his leap and gathered for a backward kick of his hind feet. The trainer follows his horse more closely than we should our wayward and frisky colt.

Fig. 100.

Fig. 101.

6

THE FRESH HORSE

Longeing is a very effective training aid for settling a fresh horse. Horses get fresh in different ways and for different reasons, so the longeing program should always be tailored to the individual at hand. When you longe a fresh horse, do not try to program his workout right away. Let him canter around first. Let him buck and play—within reason. Do not squash all his exuberance, but on the other hand do not indulge him too much. Be careful not to let him get loose. Most horses need a few minutes of relative "freedom" to bounce around before they can settle down to the work at hand. Imagine how glad you would be to get out and move around if you spent most of your life penned up in a box stall.

Some horses, particularly young horses, are much more amenable under saddle if they have had just a few minutes first on the longe line. Such a horse should be tacked up and longed briefly with his tack on. Be sure to tie up the stirrups securely (see Fig. 43), so they do not slip down and bang on his rib cage. If the reins are long enough, slip them under the stirrup irons as demonstrated in Fig. 44. Otherwise wrap them around the horse's neck or use a double snap to attach them to the D on the front of the saddle.

Whether to longe a fresh horse in a halter or to work him in side reins depends on the horse and the situation. A fresh horse can be worked down more quickly in side reins, particularly if they are tight. Longeing in a halter is a more recreational exercise, but certain fresh horses need exercise, not work. Horses that are too fresh because they have not been turned out thrive on a 20- to 30-minute romp on the longe line. Exceptionally well-balanced horses that carry themselves well without the support of being in a frame created by the side reins often do better when longed in a halter. Also opt for longeing in a halter if the person longeing the horse has not yet mastered the technique.

Old horses that know their jobs well and are just a little fresh can also be longed in a halter. Often they just need a few turns on the longe line to get the kinks out and limber up. Smart older horses should be somewhat indulged on the longe line. Usually they will tell you quite clearly when they have had enough. One old horse in our care charges around, bucking and kicking at first, then he slows to a trot, and finally he stops altogether and looks as if to say, "That's enough for today." The test is to reverse him and if he just quietly jogs around in the second direction, he has had enough. If he bucks and kicks again, he needs more work.

However, do not confuse the "foolers" with the smart older horses. Some horses will loaf around on the longe line even if you pop the whip behind them. Then under tack they are far too fresh. In short, it is very important to know the individual you are dealing with when working down a fresh horse. That is why a show horse's groom is so important to the end result. The groom establishes a

rapport with the horse and usually knows better than anyone else how fresh he is on a given day and how much work
on the longe he needs in the morning in order to make that
peak performance happen later in the ring.

When you choose to longe your fresh horse just in his
halter, bear in mind you have a lot less control over him.
If you are at all concerned that he may be too strong, run a
chain over his nose or use a longeing halter to gain more
leverage. Once a horse learns he can get away on the longe
line, he will always have that in the back of his mind, and
he will try to escape if given the chance. One very famous
show hunter we had in our barn for a while was such a case.
When we bought him we were told, "He doesn't longe."
Sure enough he *does not* longe. He is all right in a small
enclosed area, but otherwise, forget it. He escapes every
time, no matter what equipment he has on. A lovely, lovely
horse, he is one of those rare creatures that really wants to
be good all the time—except on the longe line. He found
out as a youngster that he could get away, and he is never
going to forget it. Obviously, trying to longe such a horse
is definitely not worth the risk.

Every rider beyond the beginner level should be taught
to longe his horse when the horse is too fresh to deal with
under saddle. Beginners' horses should always be properly prepared for them, but even a low intermediate rider
can sense when a horse is too fresh, and at such times he
should be able to hop off and put the horse on the longe for
a while. It gives a rider tremendous confidence to learn
early on that he can cope with a fresh horse, if not by riding
it until it is quiet, then at least by longeing it. When a horse
proves to be too fresh under tack, leave the tack on, tie up
the reins and stirrups, run the longe line through the bit
on the inside, over his poll, through the throatlatch (to
keep it from sliding back along his neck), and attach it to
the bit on the outside (see Figs. 25, 26). Work him in both
directions at all gaits until he settles down enough for you
to ride him again.

Almost all fresh horses benefit from time spent on the
longe line. Unfortunately, the longe is often abused by
zealous trainers at horse shows. When horses are traveling

Fig. 102.

Fig. 102a.

Figs. 102, 102a. *Question:* How can one built so hollow jump so round? *Answer:* Extensive training on the longe line!

"Sky High," affectionately known as Camel for obvious reasons, has spent at least 70 percent of his lifetime training time on the longe line. He is such a pro now that he will longe without the line! First David Hopper, who handled all his early training, and later Normal Dello Joio, who campaigned him successfully in Major Grand Prix for years, spent hours with Camel on the longe line to teach him to make the most of his unfortunate shape. Even now at the age of 15, Camel prepares all winter long for the Junior Jumper Division by trotting and cantering cavaletti. A capable horse, but not a freaky talent, his sweet disposition has been a real asset. Not many horses would take such rigorous training for so many years. *(Photo 102 by Philip Richter and 102A by Judith Buck/Dark Room on Wheels.)*

from show to show without any opportunity to be turned out, they can get very fresh. "L.T.D." (Longe 'Til Dead) is a phrase seen on the work lists of many big stables at horse shows. Ideally, we would all like to have horses that did not need to be worked hard in the morning in order to get a good performance later in the ring. But there are always a few that need to be "killed" in the morning, and, since riding them too long makes their backs sore, longeing is sometimes the last resort. Nevertheless, the conscientious trainer must always keep foremost in his mind the horse's physical well-being. Longeing is a very strenuous exercise for any horse, and making him lame in order to make him quiet enough to win makes no sense at all. Another important consideration is that extensive longeing makes a horse too thin and too fit, whereas show hunters are supposed to be fat and sleek. In short, finding the proper balance when longeing a fresh horse, whether at home or at a horse show, is no easy task. The horse must be quiet and well-behaved to do his job at home and in the show ring; he must look well and, last but by no means least, he must be sound.

7

THE TENSE HORSE

Often a tense horse benefits from work on the longe line, particularly a horse that has been the victim of some bad rides. This makes him fearful of what the rider is going to do to him next, and he will relax sooner if dealt with from the ground first. A tense, worried horse should be longed in a secluded place, and particular care should be taken not to alarm him. In most cases, medium-length side reins are helpful because a tense horse usually is worried about his mouth; he needs to learn to accept the bit. Sometimes quiet, steady work on the longe helps him to relax, round his back, drop his head, and accept the bit. Speaking to him in a soothing voice—"easy," "steady"—also may help to relax him. Even if the longe whip worries him at

Fig. 103. Close-up of the long rein that attaches to the girth rather than the horse's bit. This device effectively controls the hindquarters without punishing the horse's mouth.

first, do not omit carrying it, but be careful not to wave it around unnecessarily. Eventually he will learn to accept the longe whip with equanimity. You will probably not have to use it much, but just your holding it behind his hocks will prevent him from dropping back behind the bit, a favorite evasion of horses that are worried about being jabbed in the mouth. Often, ten to 20 minutes' work on the longe line makes such a horse more relaxed and more willing to accept the bit when ridden afterward.

"Hot" horses, generally nervous animals that tend to get more wound up the more they work, often do better if longed first as a warm-up. At horse shows where the schooling area is a busy place, such a horse is better off jogging around under tack for a few minutes in a quiet place. (Here again, the understanding groom is invaluable.) Horses with this tendency to get wound up need to warm up physically, but they also need to be kept as cool as possible mentally. Usually they do best with a quiet longe and a very brief school in the schooling area before going to the ring.

Mares are apt to be more temperamental than geldings and often do better if longed quietly before an important school or class at a horse show. A casual longeing serves them better sometimes than a rigorous schooling on the flat, which can make them resentful rather than supple. Also, mares as a lot are less forgiving than geldings and less likely to forget abuses from a bad rider. Their sensitivity can work to your advantage if you know how to deal with it. In general, tense horses are often the ones that try the hardest for you in the ring, but without careful preparation beforehand they fall apart easily under pressure.

Fig. 104. This modified long-reining rig was developed recently by my sister, Carol Thompson, who had a horse with a very sensitive mouth who swung his quarters out on the longe line. Using the customary side reins and longe line, she attached another longe line to the surcingle on the outside and passed it around his quarters. She holds the line in her whip hand, thereby having control over his hindquarters without interfering with his mouth. It works very well.

The Stiff Horse

The stiff horse is tense in a different way from the hot, nervous horse and from the "tough" horse (the subject of the next chapter). The stiff horse's tension is physical more than mental, although mental resistance always exists with the physical stiffness. Often a horse's stiffness is caused by physical problems. If so, call in your veterinarian and blacksmith to help you out, and do not get carried away with your training program or you may turn your stiff horse into a cripple. Stiffness also occurs because of conformation defects. Avoid buying a horse that is built like a camel or giraffe. If you fall for an oddly shaped horse because of other qualities you value, such as outstanding temperament and freaky talent, you will have your work cut out for you. Sometimes, however, you can accomplish a lot.

Usually a stiff horse will improve markedly with proper longe work. For such a horse I usually use tighter side reins, again with the inside side rein 2 to 3 inches shorter than the outside rein. Sometimes working him with the side reins between his front legs helps to soften him up. Usually he is worse in one direction than the other. Work him in the easier direction first and in the harder direction longer (approximately one-third of your work the easy way and two-thirds the harder way).

Extensive work over the cavaletti should help soften him. Work him first at the trot and then at the canter.

Usually a horse's stiffness shows up most clearly at the canter on the longe. A stiff horse tends to cross-canter; he will be on one lead in front and the other lead behind. When he cross-canters, try making the circle larger until he gets his balance better. Every time he cross-canters, try to let him jog a step or two to get him to change up. In the early stages, chasing him with the whip to force a flying change usually makes him more stiff and tense, so he ends up charging around faster and faster, still at the cross canter. (Later, when he is more supple, often a flick of the whip is enough to get him to change up.)

Work over cavaletti really helps the stiff, chronic cross-cantering horse. Hopping over the cavaletti helps to make him more limber, and as he canters the last cavaletto, encourage him to land on the correct lead with a slight pull on the longe line. Stiff horses do not give up the cross canter easily, certainly not in one session. However, if you persevere, most of them will come around. Reward him with your voice if he does happen to catch the lead— "Good boy"—to let him know you are pleased. Do not let him stop cantering—as some are apt to do—at the tiniest word of praise!

Be careful that you do not, in your zeal, overwork the stiff horse. As he gets more tired, he will at least seem to get more limber. For him especially, longeing is physically exhausting because he is using muscles he has not used before. For an unfit horse, ten to 15 minutes is enough. A fit horse can take 20 to 30 minutes if rested a few times during the session. Be satisfied with a little progress each day. You are not going to make him supple in one session, and if you do too much you risk breaking him down.

THE TOUGH HORSE

The "tough" horse is stiff and tense, but he is tough as well. His resistance is mental as well as physical, mental even more than physical. Rather than "having it out" with him under saddle, you are often better off letting him fight himself on the longe. Then you can get on him and be "Mr. Nice Guy."

The tough horse does not give in easily; some of them never come around. Persistent training can improve most tough horses, however. Sometimes the really good competitive horses are tough in the beginning, especially if they have had bad training. But if you have one of those that simply refuse to come around, get rid of him. The time you waste trying to make a good horse out of him would be better used training two or three nice horses that want to be good horses.

The tough horse has a strong will and often a temper as well. Do not let his temper rouse yours. Though you may have several long sessions on the longe line with him at first, do not develop a pattern of exhausting him to make him give in. You are only fooling yourself that he is making progress when in fact he is simply too exhausted to resist. You may have the upper hand physically for a while, but you have probably not won him over mentally. You are making him fitter and fitter and probably tougher and tougher. Also, there is always the risk of breaking him down. As a rule of thumb, any more than 30 minutes on the longe line is probably too long and will not accomplish much in the end. The tough horse—indeed, any horse— has to learn to do what you want him to do because he wants to do it.

How then do you get him to give in and want to do it your way? His whole program should be carefully monitored. A tough horse characteristically has a lot of excess energy, even more than the average horse. He needs to spend a lot of time in the paddock. It is almost impossible to bring around a tough horse without giving him plenty of turnout time. Furthermore, he may need to live on hay for a while; omit his grain ration, which only serves to increase his already excessive energy. Give him all the hay he will eat to prevent loss of weight and condition, and once he settles into the program slowly start him back on grain.

Before starting to longe him, make sure that you have the upper hand from the outset. Work in an enclosed area. Make extra sure all the equipment is sturdy. A tough horse should never learn that he can escape or break the equipment. I usually work a tough horse in a more restricted frame: shorter side reins and/or Chambon or DeGogue. Be ready to counteract his resistance to the side reins by driving him forward with the longe whip *before* he stops or runs backwards. Be stern with him, but praise him extravagantly when he starts to come around. Persistent and patient training on the longe line improves most tough horses and makes them more tractable when ridden.

Fig. 105. Here the horse is outfitted with an overcheck and side reins. The overcheck in this picture is too long to do any good. It should be almost snug when the horse is standing with his normal head carriage. The overcheck prevents the horse from overflexing and hiding behind the bit. It can be used over cavaletti but not over jumps since it would punish the horse for lowering his head and trying to round his back over the jump.

Fig. 106. Here the side reins are attached to the surcingle between the horse's legs. This is an extreme measure to get a tough horse to give in quickly. These reins, however, are still not as confining as the Chambon and the DeGogue martingale. Attached as shown here and with an insistent driving whip from behind, they are effective in making a tough horse give in and round his back.

Fig. 107.

Figs. 107, 108. The Chambon and the DeGogue are French devices for inducing a horse to lower his head and stretch his neck. Although they do not really substitute for proper training, they are helpful in an emergency when time is short and a very rigid horse needs softening up. Horses tend to rebel strongly against both these devices when first used, so you must take care from the start to prevent an accident. Never attach either device until the horse is out of the barn and then attach it only loosely at first. The Chambon goes from the bit through a pulley at the horse's poll and back down between his front legs to the girth. As the horse raises his head it becomes taut and exerts pressure on his poll: as the horse lowers his head it loosens up and rewards him. In both of these pictures the Chambon is loosely adjusted, thus encouraging the horse to lower his head rather than forcing him to do so.

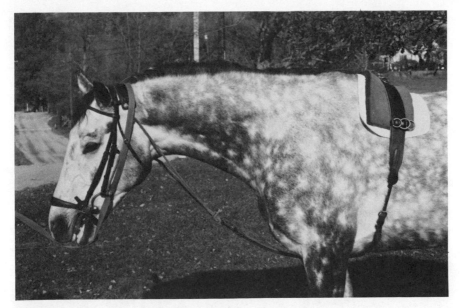

Fig. 108.

Fig. 109. This DeGogue is properly adjusted. Instead of fastening to the bit as the Chambon does, the DeGogue passes through the bit and attaches to itself at the horse's chest. The DeGogue and the Chambon can be handy shortcuts that help with a very tough horse in a given situation, but when used excessively they often make a horse more rigid and defensive. Both must be used with considerable caution. Even when loosely attached they are very confining, and horses often will rebel strongly against them, running backwards, rearing, and even falling down. These devices are *not* for neophytes and should always be accompanied by an encouraging whip from behind.

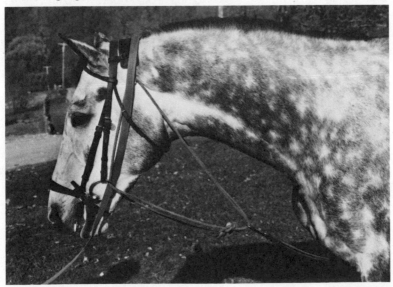

Fig. 110.

Figs. 110–112. This longeing rig is so new that it doesn't even have a proper name yet; most simply call it "the ropes." Developed simultaneously in Europe by Nelson Pessoa and in the United States by David Hopper, it has quickly become very popular, particularly with trainers and riders of jumpers, who find it very helpful in softening up tough horses. Apparently it encourages them to get round without making them too mad. These ropes are attached between the front legs, pass through the bit, through the surcingle rings, and around the horse's hindquarters. A rope from the top of the surcingle keeps the hindquarter rope from slipping down. This rig can be constructed easily with clothesline. Cover the part of the rope that goes around the haunches with sheepskin halter tubing. Like the Chambon and the DeGogue, "the ropes" should not be too tight at first. *(Photos by Philip Richter.)*

Fig. 111.

Fig. 112.

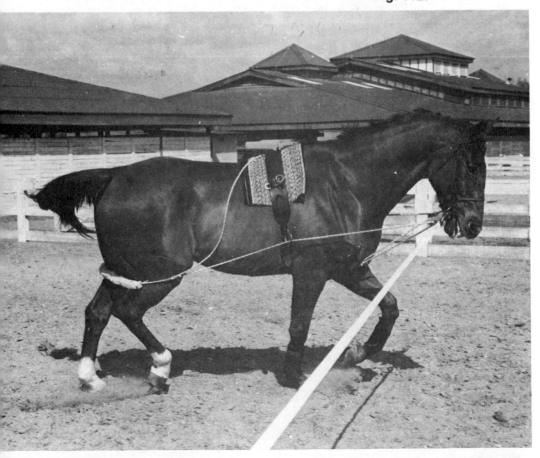

How and When To Pick a Fight

As a general rule, try to arrange the horse's lesson so that everything goes smoothly. Horses learn best in a simple, straightforward program. Occasionally, however, with a tough horse it is advantageous to pick a fight with him in order to establish authority. It is of paramount importance to arrange the situation so that he has to do what you want even though he does not want to. First and foremost, stage the encounter in an enclosed area, so that he cannot get away. You may choose to omit the morning turnout that usually makes him more amenable. Reverse the usual procedure in the longeing area. Work him in the difficult direction first. Insist that he do the cavaletti exercise going away from the barn or in-gate. Be a little casual about staying behind him with the whip. Then if he does balk, corner him and get right after him with the whip until he marches around the way he is supposed to. Do not let his temper rouse yours; keep the punishment calm and methodical. When he does the designated exercise properly, praise him extravagantly.

The ancient Greek horseman Xenophon had a good understanding of the tough horse. He points out that "mettle is to a horse what temper is to a man." He urges us to "avoid fretting a high-mettled horse" and hence not exasperate him. His conclusion that "the most ambitious horses are the highest-mettled" still holds true today. When the right program is used, tough horses can become the best competitors of all.

COMPETITION HORSES

A horse's longeing program may be crucial to his competition effort. Whether he wins or loses may well be determined by if, how, and when he was longed before the event. A trainer's attention to such details is essential for success in competition. Often it is a horse's groom that knows best how to prepare his charge on the longe line to bring him to his peak for the competition at hand.

Most top competitive horses, no matter how good their dispositions, are as a rule good-feeling, exuberant horses, so many of them do need preparation either on the longe or under tack before major competitions.

At one end of the spectrum there is the "L.T.D." (Longe 'Til Dead) candidate. He really needs to be "killed" on the

Fig. 113.

Figs. 113–114. Here is a good example of recreational longe-ing. The intention here is to freshen up a stale horse that has just finished a long morning of demonstrating for this book. We took off all the paraphernalia—side reins, surcingle, Chambon, DeGogue—and slipped his halter on with a chain over his nose for more control. We sent him around on an extra long longe line

Fig. 114.

(actually, two lines tied together) in this big open field, and look at the change in him after a couple of laps around! In **Fig. 113** he looks pretty sour and bored. In **Fig. 114** he's beginning to freshen up and enjoy himself. Likewise, a horse that is used to being turned out every day at home really misses that freedom when he's on the road showing every weekend. A few minutes of pseudo freedom does wonders for his frame of mind.

Fig. 115. Longeing on the side of a hill makes an interesting variation for sound, well-balanced horses. For colts, this kind of exercise up hill and down dale is too difficult. For them, just organizing themselves on a circle is enough. A horse that has a tendency to pitch on his front end would also have problems dealing with a hill.

Fig. 116. After he has finished his work, you should let him graze for a few minutes, but let that be *your* decision, not his. Even during a recreational longeing session, you do not want him sauntering around and grabbing mouthfuls of grass at random.

longe line to perform well in the ring. The rider has to learn to cope to some extent with such a horse, however, because sooner or later soundness problems will occur if the horse is always "killed" on the longe.

When putting together new horse-and-rider combinations, especially juniors and amateurs with new horses, the horse must be extra quiet because the rider is extra nervous with the excitement of competing on a new horse. In most cases, the capable trainer can develop the rider's confidence and skill, so eventually the horse does not have to be "killed" to make a winning combination.

Another competition horse that thrives on judicious longeing is the very tense horse. Before an important event he may do better jogging around for a few minutes to warm up in a quiet corner rather than entering the fray of the schooling area under saddle. The less he sees of the hectic schooling area, the less frazzled he will be when he gets to the ring.

A sour or cranky horse also benefits from a nice casual romp on the longe, whether it is early in the morning or just before the competition. After spending weeks on the road without being turned out, a loose longe on a long line, or even two longe lines tied together giving him a diameter of 120 feet instead of 60 feet to play in, helps to sweeten him up. Since a cranky horse is often irritated by other horses in a crowded schooling area, he may warm up in a better frame of mind if longed in a quiet corner before an important competition.

Stiff and/or old horses often perform better if they have an opportunity to loosen up a bit on the longe line before they compete. Often such horses will let you know when they have had enough longeing.

When preparing a horse for competition, it is especially important that a trainer have an understanding of the horse's mentality as well as his physical needs as he plans the longeing program for the day. Here again the horse's groom is invaluable, if he knows his horse and rider well.

10

HORSES NOT TO LONGE

Because longeing is a very strenuous exercise, a rigorous longeing program does not work in some instances. Be particularly careful about longeing older horses. They should not be asked to work in very short, tight circles. Too often a slightly overzealous longeing session turns a "serviceably sound" older horse into a lame pensioner for life.

A tough horse with known soundness problems also poses a real dilemma. He needs the work on the longe line, but physically he cannot take it. Monitoring such a horse's program is not easy. Standing him in the stall for an hour or two in the bitting rig may help a little, but whoever rides him had better be prepared to cope with his toughness.

Afterword

Proper work on the longe line will improve most horses. It is not a panacea nor is it an adequate substitute for a thoughtful schooling on the flat or over jumps. Longeing can coordinate well in certain stages of a horse's life and in certain emergency situations. Longeing a young horse is the very best and most logical introduction for him to work under saddle. A fresh horse is much more amenable after a quick romp on the longe line. Stiff, tense, tough, and spoiled horses almost always improve with a thoughtful longeing program. Horses that develop sore backs or girth galls can be kept fit on the longe line. If a good rider is not readily available, a lot can be accomplished by longeing.

It is an interesting paradox that we continually work our

horses on the circle so that we may ultimately ride them straight. Longeing is an effective means for teaching a horse to go forward and straight. The horse learns to cooperate with the trainer on the longe line, and this spirit of cooperation helps him ultimately to yield to his rider because he *wants* to yield, not because he feels coerced.

Index

Assistant, in longeing process, 34–35, 48–51, 78

Bell boots, 20, 21
Berenger, Richard, 4
Bit(s), 41, 77
   introduction of, to horse, 39, 40
   types of, 17
Bridle, 17
   on colts, 45
   introduction of, to horse, 17, 38, 39, 48

Camel, 100
Cantering, 51, 58
   over cavaletti, 14, 64, 68, 84, 87
   of stiff horse, 106–107
Capriole, 94

Cavaletti, 12–16, 59–67, 74
   cantering over, 14, 64, 68, 84, 87
   common evasions at, 67
   at full height, 60–66
   in jumps, 72
   setting up, 14, 16
   stacking of, 15, 65
   for stiff horse, 106, 107
   for tough horse, 116
   trotting over, 14, 15, 60, 61, 68, 84, 87
Chain, on colt, 45
Chain shank, 41
Chambon, 110, 112–114
Classical training, longeing in, 5
Colts, 78
   chains on, 45
   fully tacked up, 49
Common evasion on longe line, 55–57

INDEX

Competition horses, 117–123
The Compleat Horseman, 4
Concentration span, of horse, 52
Conformation defects, in stiff horse, 106
Cranky horse, 123
Cross-canter, of stiff horse, 106–107

de la Gueriniere, 4
DeGogue, 110, 112–114
Dello Joio, Normal, 100
Drop noseband, 19

Egg-butt bit, 17
Egg-butt snaffle, 39
Equipment, 12–16; *see also individual
    entries*
Exercise, tailoring to horse's needs, 66

Flying changes, 86
Foot gear, 21
Footing, in longeing area, 10–11
Fresh horse, 97–101
    longeing just in halter, 99
    side reins versus halter for, 98
Full hind boots, 23

Geldings, temperament of, 105
Grass, in longeing area, 11
Grazing, 122
Groom, horse and, 98–99
Ground, in longeing area, 10
Ground lines, 74
"Gumdrop bit," 17

Hacksmore, 77
Halter, 40, 41
    on colt, 45
    on fresh horse, 98
Hillsides, longeing on, 121
Hind boots, 20
A History of Horsemanship, 4
Hollow-mouth loose-ring, 39
Hope, Sir William, 4
Hopper, David, 100, 114
Horse
    concentration span of, 52
    equipment for, 17–35; *see also
        individual entries*
    framing of, 52
Horses's legs, protection of, 21
Horses not to longe, 125
"Hot" horses, 105

Jannell, Joe, 67
"Jumping round," 75
Jumps, *see* Longeing over jumps, Low
    jumps

Lean pole, 68
    purposes of, 69
Leather hind ankle boots, 22
Lipizzaner stallions, 94
Location, for longeing, 8–9, 69
Long-reining
    advantages of, over longeing,
        85
    of colts, 78
    of older horses, 79–84
Long reins, 77–84
    advantage of, 79
    attached to girth, 104
    candidates for, 84
    in flying changes, 86
    in going straight, 91
    jumping horses in, 87
    for lateral work, 92
    for older horse, 78
    reversing of, 80
    in trotting, 86, 91
Longe, as term, 3
Longe line, 17, 30
    arranging, 31, 33
    attached to noseband, 79
    chain end of, 46
    of horse traveling left, 34
    lengthening and shortening of,
        58
    reasons for training on, 7
    rubber disk on, 33
    as supplement training under saddle,
        7
Longe-line work, as exercise, 8
Longe 'Til Dead, *see* "L.T.D."
Longe whip, 17, 34, 51, 56, 75, 79–84,
        103–105
    introduction of, to horse, 51
    pointing of, 50
    and tough horse, 110, 116
Longeing
    advantages of, 127–128
    history of, 4–5
    location for, 8–9
    principles of, 7
Longeing cavesson, 43, 77
Longeing over jumps, 69, 74
    purpose of, 16, 68
Loose-ring hollow-mouth snaffle, 17, 18
Low jumps, 59, 68–75
"L.T.D." (Longe 'Til Dead), 101, 117–123

Mares, temperament of, 105
Metal D bit, 17, 18
Modified long-reining rig, 105

Noseband, 19, 79

130

Old horses, 123
  of fresh nature, 98
  long-reining of, 78, 79–84
Open-front shin boots, 21
Overcheck, 111
Oxer, 72, 74–75

Pesoa, Nelson, 114
Polo wraps, 20, 22, 23
Preparation, for longeing, 7–35

Recreational longeing, 118–119
Reins, see Side reins
Relaxing influence, longeing as, 9
"The ropes," 114
Rubber D bit, 79

Saddle, introduction to horse, 39
Safety, on longe line, 11–12
Screw-in caulks, 20
Shin boots, 20–22
Side reins, 17, 24, 26, 28, 111
  for fresh horse, 98
  for stiff horse, 106
  for tough horse, 110
  unhitching of, 52
  for young horse, 29
"Sky High," 100
Sour horse, 123
Stiff horse, 106–107, 123

Stirrups, 98
  on colt, 49
Suppling exercises, 57–58, 87, 92
Surcingle, 17, 24, 26, 29
  introduction of, to horse, 39, 48

Tense horse, 103–107
Terry Lad, 67
Thompson, Carol, 105
Timing, of longeing sessions, 10, 52
  for fresh horses, 99–101
  for stiff horses, 107
Tough horse, 109–116
  longe whip and, 110, 116
  picking a fight with, 116
  side reins and, 110
Trench, Charles Chevenix, 4
Trotting, 51, 58
  over cavaletti, 14, 15, 60, 61, 68, 84, 87
  long reins in, 86, 91

Vertical, 74–75
Very tense horse, 123

Walking, 51, 58
Weather, and longeing sessions, 11
Working gaits, 58

Young horse, 37–52
  purpose of longeing, 37

131